About
Skill Builders
Reading
Comprehension
Grade 8
by Jerry Aten

Welcome to the Skill Builders series. This series is designed to make learning both fun and rewarding.

This workbook offers a balanced mixture of humor, imagination, and instruction as students steadily improve their reading comprehension skills. The diverse assignments in this workbook are designed to enhance basic reading skills while giving students something fun to think about—from honeybees to coral reefs.

Additionally, a critical thinking section includes exercises to help develop higher-order thinking skills.

Learning is more effective when approached with enthusiasm. That's why the Skill Builders series combines entertaining and academically sound exercises with engaging graphics and exciting themes—to make reviewing basic skills at school or at home fun and effective, for both you and your budding scholars.

Credits:
Editor: Julie Kirsch
Layout Design: Mark Conrad
Illustrations: Jim Nuttle
Cover Concept: Nick Greenwood

www.summerbridgeactivities.com

Printed in the USA • All rights reserved.   ISBN: 978-1-60022-148-4

Table of Contents

Suggested Reading List............3

Jesse's Gold 4

The Rescue of JFK 6

The Great Bambino...............8

Analyzing Poetry:

    Emily Dickinson 10

Billie Jean King 12

Alquerque 14

Sue Hendrickson 16

Man with a Dream 18

Two Years in Hiding 20

The Berlin Wall..................22

The Play's the Thing 24

The Smithville Gazette...........26

Alcatraz 28

Myths, Legends, and Folktales 30

Conquering Mount Everest.......32

The Watergate Scandal...........34

Who Discovered America? 36

Aloha!...........................38

Woodstock 1969 40

Chief Joseph 42

Underwater "Cities" 44

Analyzing Poetry: Robert Frost....46

James Meredith 48

Johnny Appleseed...............50

Maria Montessori 52

Sooners.........................54

Skin Deep.......................56

Dancing Honeybees 58

Robert Peary....................60

Digital Cameras 62

Returned to China...............64

Arlington National Cemetery.....66

Sonnets.........................68

Critical Thinking Skills 71

    The Odd Word Out 71

    Fractured Phrases............72

    Oxymorons 73

    Analogies 74

    Rebus Puzzles 75

Answer Key 77

© Rainbow Bridge Publishing   *Reading Comprehension* • RB-904060

Suggested Reading List

Aiken, Joan
  Midnight Is a Place

Avi
  Nothing but the Truth

Barron, T. A.
  The Ancient One

Bradbury, Ray
  Fahrenheit 451

Brashares, Ann
  The Sisterhood of the Traveling Pants series

Burnford, Shelia
  The Incredible Journey

Choi, Sook Nyul
  Year of Impossible Goodbyes

de Trevino, Elizabeth Borton
  I, Juan de Pareja

du Bois, William Pène
  The Twenty-One Balloons

Field, Rachel
  Calico Bush

Fitzgerald, F. Scott
  The Great Gatsby

Forbes, Esther
  Paul Revere and the World He Lived In

Gannett, Ruth Stiles
  My Father's Dragon

Gray, Elizabeth Janet
  Adam of the Road

Haddix, Margaret Peterson
  Among the Hidden

Hemingway, Ernest
  The Old Man and the Sea

Hoffman, Alice
  Green Angel

Holm, Anne
  I Am David

Jackson, Shirley
  The Haunting of Hill House

Kelly, Eric P.
  The Trumpeter of Krakow

Keyes, Daniel
  Flowers for Algernon

Koller, Jackie French
  Nothing to Fear

Lee, Harper
  To Kill a Mockingbird

London, Jack
  White Fang

Lyons, Mary E.
  Letters from a Slave Girl: The Story of Harriet Jacobs

Merrill, Jean
  The Pushcart War

McCloskey, Robert
  Homer Price

McKinley, Robin
  The Blue Sword

O'Dell, Scott
  Island of the Blue Dolphins; The Black Pearl

Paulsen, Gary
  The Haymeadow

Pullman, Philip
  The Ruby in the Smoke

Rottman, S. L.
  Rough Waters

Temple, Frances
  Taste of Salt: A Story of Modern Haiti

Thesman, Jean
  When the Road Ends

Whelan, Gloria
  Listening for Lions

© Rainbow Bridge Publishing

Reading Comprehension • RB-904060

Jesse's Gold

The 1936 Olympic Games were held in Berlin, Germany. These Olympics gave Adolf Hitler a chance to showcase the new Germany. Hitler thought that white Germans were better athletes than people from other nations, and he hoped the Olympic Games would prove his theories of racial superiority.

Hitler built a *grandiose* facility to host the Olympic Games. He wanted to make these games the best ever. He was convinced that German athletes would dominate the games. What he did not know was that an African American athlete from the United States was about to surprise the world.

Jesse Owens won his first gold medal in the 100-meter dash when he matched the world record of 10.3 seconds. The gold medal winner of the 100-meter dash is considered the "world's fastest human." Hitler was so upset that he refused to attend the medal ceremony. Jesse won his second gold medal in the long jump. He set an Olympic record. He also won a gold medal in the 200-meter dash, when he set a new Olympic record of 20.7 seconds. He won his fourth gold medal as a member of the United States 4 x 100-meter relay team. The win set a world record at 39.8 seconds. Even the German people applauded Jesse's performances.

Jesse Owens returned to the United States as a hero. He was the first American athlete ever to win four gold medals in the Olympic Games. In speaking of his Olympic success, Owens said, "It dawned on me with blinding brightness. I realized: I had jumped into another rare kind of stratosphere—one that only a handful of people in every generation are lucky enough to know."

© Rainbow Bridge Publishing *Reading Comprehension* • RB-904060

Reading Comprehension

1. In which of the following Olympic events did Jesse Owens not win a gold medal?
   A. pole vault
   B. long jump
   C. 100-meter dash
   D. 200-meter dash

2. Choose another good title for the reading.
   A. Jesse's Defeat
   B. A Gold Medal Game
   C. The Triumph of Track and Field
   D. The Rise of Nazi Germany

3. Which of the following best defines the word *grandiose*?
   A. spectacular
   B. moderate
   C. modern
   D. conservative

4. Which of the following events happened second?
   A. The German people applauded Jesse.
   B. Jesse Owens returned to the United States as a hero.
   C. Jesse Owens won the 100-meter dash and was considered the "world's fastest human."
   D. Hitler wanted to prove that white Germans were a superior race.

5. What do you think Jesse Owens meant when he said that he had "jumped into another rare kind of stratosphere—one that only a handful of people in every generation are lucky enough to know."

   _____

   _____

   _____

   _____

The Rescue of JFK

During World War II, Lieutenant John F. Kennedy (JFK) was in charge of a torpedo boat named *PT-109*. The boat was stationed near the Solomon Islands in the South Pacific. In 1943, a Japanese destroyer rammed into the *PT-109*, cutting Kennedy's boat in half. As *PT-109* gradually sank, Kennedy and 10 other crew members abandoned the ship and began swimming to a nearby island. The future president spent nearly 15 hours helping the survivors to nearby Plum Pudding Island. He then led the crew members in what would become a week-long struggle for survival.

Finding no food or water on Plum Pudding Island, the men swam to Olasana and Nauru Islands in search of help. They found very little on the deserted islands. The crew lived off coconuts for six days. Fortunately, a coast watcher had seen the explosion. Coast watchers were Australian *expatriates* who operated secretly behind Japanese lines. They warned Allied forces of approaching Japanese forces. The coast watcher who saw the explosion contacted two native scouts—Eroni Kumana and Biuku Gasa.

Kumana and Gasa were searching for survivors when they found Kennedy and his men. Kennedy scratched a message on the inside of a coconut husk. The two scouts delivered the message to an Australian military unit in the area. A short time later, Kennedy and his men were rescued.

Kennedy promised Kumana and Gasa that he would meet them again. When he was elected president, Kennedy invited the men to the White House for the presidential inauguration. However, when they arrived at the island airport, they were not allowed to leave because they did not speak English. Almost 60 years later—and about 40 years after the president's death—Kennedy's nephew went to the island to meet Kumana and Gasa. His visit showed that their brave actions had not been forgotten.

© Rainbow Bridge Publishing *Reading Comprehension • RB-904060*

Reading Comprehension

1. During World War II, Lieutenant John F. Kennedy was stationed in the
   A. North Atlantic.
   B. Adriatic Sea.
   C. Indian Ocean.
   D. South Pacific.

2. Which of the following best defines the word *expatriate*?
   A. traitor
   B. renegade
   C. resident living in a foreign land
   D. smuggler

3. Number the following events in the order that they happened.

   _____ The survivors of *PT-109* swam to Plum Pudding Island.

   _____ Kennedy's torpedo boat was destroyed.

   _____ The survivors of the *PT-109* were found by two natives.

   _____ Kennedy's nephew met with his uncle's rescuers.

   _____ Kennedy scratched a message on a coconut shell.

4. Which of these statements is true?
   A. A Japanese destroyer sank *PT-109*.
   B. Kennedy and his crew were rescued three days after *PT-109* sank.
   C. Two scouts delivered Kennedy's message to an American military unit in the area.
   D. Kennedy's message was written on a palm-tree leaf.

5. Why do you think Kumana and Gasa risked their lives to rescue Kennedy and his surviving crew?

   _____

   _____

   _____

   _____

The Great Bambino

George Herman Ruth has long been a famous baseball hero. When Ruth was seven years old, his father placed him in an orphanage. While he was there, he played many different positions on the baseball team. His two favorite positions were catcher and pitcher.

When Ruth was 19 years old, Jack Dunn, owner of the Baltimore Orioles, recognized his talent. Dunn had a reputation for helping young players with their careers. When players saw Ruth with Dunn, they referred to him as "Jack's newest babe." The name "Babe" caught on and became his nickname.

After a few months with the Orioles, a minor league team at the time, Ruth made it to the major leagues with the Boston Red Sox. While he was in Boston, Ruth broke many records for pitching and hitting home runs. After six years, he was traded to the New York Yankees. He became the greatest attraction in baseball, and Yankee Stadium became known as "the house that Ruth built."

Ruth set records that stood for decades. In 1927, he hit 60 home runs during a single season. Writers attempted to capture a sense of his greatness by giving him catchy nicknames. He was called "The Great Bambino" and the "Sultan of Swat." Ruth and his teammate Lou Gehrig were a *dynamic* duo of home-run hitters. During his 22 seasons in the major leagues, Ruth hit a record 714 home runs. Ruth also had a lifetime batting average of .342.

When Babe Ruth died of cancer in 1948, his coffin was placed at the entrance to Yankee Stadium. Thousands of fans filed past to say good-bye to their beloved hero.

© Rainbow Bridge Publishing Reading Comprehension • RB-904060

Reading Comprehension

1. Babe Ruth spent most of his major league career as a member of which of these baseball teams?
   A. Baltimore Orioles
   B. New York Yankees
   C. Boston Red Sox
   D. Chicago Cubs

2. Which of these statements is not true?
   A. Ruth spent much of his childhood in an orphanage.
   B. Ruth hit 714 major league home runs.
   C. Ruth was nicknamed Babe Ruth after a popular candy bar.
   D. During his youth, Ruth played many different positions.

3. Which of the following events happened first?
   A. Ruth hit 60 home runs in a single season.
   B. Ruth was traded to the New York Yankees.
   C. Ruth signed a contract with the Baltimore Orioles.
   D. Ruth pitched for the Boston Red Sox.

4. Which of the following best defines the word *dynamic*?
   A. helpful
   B. powerful
   C. motivated
   D. friendly

5. Why do you think fans were so devoted to Babe Ruth?

   _____

   _____

   _____

   _____

   _____

© Rainbow Bridge Publishing   *Reading Comprehension* • RB-904060

Analyzing Poetry

Emily Dickinson

Although Emily Dickinson spent most of her life in seclusion, her poetry made her one of the most famous American poets of all time. Before she died at the age of 55, Dickinson was a prolific poet. She wrote almost 1,800 poems. Only seven of these poems were published during her lifetime. When Dickinson's poems were published *posthumously* in a series of collections, her popularity as a poet began to grow. Initially, publishers corrected Dickinson's unusual punctuation and capitalization. Later, editors and scholars stopped changing Dickinson's poetry. Over time, her unusual use of dashes and capitalization has become a hallmark of her writing.

219

1   She sweeps with many-colored Brooms –
2   And leaves the Shreds behind –
3   Oh Housewife in the Evening West –
4   Come back, and dust the Pond!

5   You dropped a Purple Ravelling in –
6   You dropped an Amber thread –
7   And now you've littered all the East
8   With Duds of Emerald!

9   And still, she plies her spotted Brooms,
10 And still the Aprons fly,
11 Till Brooms fade softly into stars –
12 And then I come away –

© Rainbow Bridge Publishing

Reading Comprehension

1. In poem "219," Dickinson compares a woman cleaning house to
   A. the sunset.
   B. a lake.
   C. some stars.
   D. feathers.

2. Who is the "she" in the poem? What clues does Dickinson provide to help you figure this out?

   _____

   _____

   _____

3. Dickinson is famous for her unusual use of dashes and capitalization. Why do you think she did this?

   _____

   _____

   _____

4. Which of the following best defines the word *posthumously*?
   A. published by a big group of people
   B. published in a big book of poetry
   C. made public after a person has died
   D. stolen and then published

5. Find another poem by Emily Dickinson on the Internet or at your school or local library. On a separate sheet of paper, compare the two poems. How are the two poems similar? Do they share common themes, imagery, or stylistic elements (such as unusual capitalization)?

© Rainbow Bridge Publishing   *Reading Comprehension* • RB-904060

Billie Jean King

In an athletic career that spanned decades, tennis star Billie Jean King won 695 matches. She captured 39 Grand Slam titles. She was ranked number one in the world five times. However, many people remember King because of a single tennis match. On September 20, 1973, over 30,000 people crowded into the Houston Astrodome to watch King play Bobby Riggs, a former male Wimbledon champion. Approximately 50 million television viewers around the world also watched the match.

Even though she was nervous, King played confidently and easily defeated Riggs. King's victory in the match over Riggs is considered an important moment in the history of women's sports. By defeating Riggs, King showed the world that female athletes should not be underestimated. She also proved that women could thrive in pressure-filled situations.

King began playing tennis professionally in 1968. At the time, professional female athletes earned much less money than professional male athletes. This outraged King. She believed that women players should receive the same prize money as their male counterparts. In 1973, King threatened to *boycott* a major tournament unless equal prize money was offered. She suggested that other female players would do the same. In late August of that year, the U.S. Open became the first major tennis tournament to offer equal prize money to its male and female champions.

In 1974, King founded *WomenSports* magazine, the Women's Sports Foundation, and World Team Tennis. She continued to be one of the world's top tennis players. Though she retired from tennis in 1984, King remains active in the sport as a coach and sports commentator.

© Rainbow Bridge Publishing

Reading Comprehension • RB-904060

Reading Comprehension

1. Fill in the blanks to complete the time line of Billie Jean King's career.

    _____ : Billie Jean King began playing tennis professionally.

    _____ : The U.S. Open offered equal prize money to male and female champions.

    _____ : Billie Jean King defeated Bobby Riggs.

    _____ : Billie Jean King founded *WomenSports* magazine, the Women's Sports Foundation, and World Team Tennis.

    _____ : Billie Jean King retired from playing professional tennis.

2. Which of the following best defines the word *boycott*?
    A. organize a rally
    B. refuse to play
    C. play well
    D. file a lawsuit

3. Why was King's victory over Bobby Riggs an important moment in the history of athletics?

    _____

    _____

    _____

4. Which of the following statements is true?
    A. King only wanted to get rich.
    B. King was never ranked higher than third in the world.
    C. King retired from tennis and then disappeared.
    D. King proved that female athletes should not be underestimated.

5. Think of another athlete who has made a significant contribution to sports. Why is this athlete important? Continue your answer on a separate sheet of paper if necessary.

    _____

    _____

    _____

Alquerque

Alquerque (pronounced ahl-CARE-kay) is a two-player board game that originated in Egypt. It is similar to checkers.

Materials: Game board, 12 playing pieces each of two different colors

The object of the game: Players attempt to capture their opponent's pieces by jumping over them.

To play: Players should sit facing each other with the board between them. The playing pieces are arranged in the following manner:

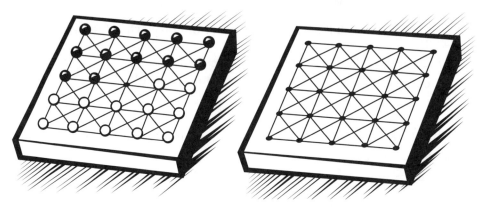

Toss a coin to determine which player moves first. Players must move their pieces along the lines of the board. Depending on which space a playing piece occupies, a player may move the piece horizontally, vertically, or diagonally. Pieces can also move forward or backward. Unless it is capturing an opponent's piece, a piece can move only one space at a time.

Capturing pieces: A player may capture an opponent's piece if the piece is sitting beside the player's piece and if the space beyond the opponent's piece is vacant. To take a piece, jump over it into the empty space. Remove the captured piece from the board. If a player captures an opponent's piece, he may take another turn. He may continue to take turns as long as he can capture pieces. Players can also choose not to move after capturing a piece. The game is over when a player has captured all of his opponent's pieces or when no more captures can be made by either player. The winner is the player with most captured pieces.

Reading Comprehension • RB-904060

Reading Comprehension

1. Look at the Alquerque boards (page 14). Consider a strategy that you would use to help you win a game. Explain why you think this strategy might be effective.

   _____

   _____

   _____

2. A piece can move
   A. two spaces at a time.
   B. only forward and diagonally.
   C. only when jumping over an opponent's piece.
   D. forward, backward, horizontally, and diagonally.

3. What two conditions must be met before a player can capture an opponent's piece?

   _____

   _____

4. Read each of the following sentences. If the sentence is true, write **T** in the space beside it. If the sentence is false, write **F**. If a sentence is false, correct the sentence to make it true.

   _____ Alquerque is a two player game.

   _____ The game is over when a player gets two pieces to the opposite end of the board.

   _____ Players must move again after capturing an opponent's piece.

   _____ Alquerque is similar to chess.

   _____ Players must move their pieces along the lines of the board.

© Rainbow Bridge Publishing

Reading Comprehension • RB-904060

Sue Hendrickson

On August 12, 1990, Sue Hendrickson made an amazing discovery on a remote cliff in South Dakota. Hendrickson, a self-trained *paleontologist*, marine *archaeologist*, and explorer, discovered the fossilized remains of an enormous *Tyrannosaurus rex*.

Hendrickson noticed a few pieces of bone on the ground as she was walking around the base of the cliff. She looked up and saw three large bones from a dinosaur's spine located about eight feet above her head. After taking a closer look at the bones, Hendrickson decided that they must have belonged to a huge *T. rex*. Her colleagues confirmed her identification of the bones when Hendrickson brought them to the site. They named the dinosaur "Sue" in honor of the woman who discovered her.

The first *T. rex* skeleton was discovered in 1900. Since then, only seven skeletons have been discovered that are at least half complete. Of these seven skeletons, Sue is the largest, best preserved, and most complete specimen. Though she died around 67 million years ago, scientists are still able to see where Sue's tendons, muscles, and other soft tissues attached to her bones. Today, Sue is on display at The Field Museum in Chicago, Illinois.

Sue's skeleton is only one of Hendrickson's exciting discoveries. While working in Peru, Hendrickson and her team of fossil hunters uncovered the fossilized remains of enormous whales. In 1992, Hendrickson joined a diving team headed by Franck Goddio, a well-known underwater archaeologist. She helped excavate a 400-year-old sunken ship full of gold and other treasures. Later, Hendrickson helped Goddio uncover Cleopatra's royal quarters in Alexandria, Egypt. An earthquake in the fourth century caused the famous Egyptian queen's summer home to sink beneath the sea. Hendrickson helped recover precious artifacts that had not been seen for over a millennium.

Reading Comprehension

1. Why was Sue Hendrickson's discovery of a fossilized *Tyrannosaurus rex* an important archeological find?

   _____

   _____

   _____

2. Judging from the context, the word *paleontologist* most likely means
   A. a scientist who studies the creation and formation of rocks.
   B. a scientist who studies the fossilized remains of plants and animals.
   C. a scientist who explores underwater shipwrecks.
   D. a treasure hunter who searches for gold in underwater shipwrecks.

3. Explain the difference between a *paleontologist* and an *archaeologist*. Use the Internet, a dictionary, or an encyclopedia if you need help.

   _____

   _____

   _____

4. Number the following events in the order that they happened.

   _____ An earthquake caused Cleopatra's royal quarters to sink beneath the sea.

   _____ Sue Hendrickson discovered the remains of an enormous *Tyrannosaurus rex*.

   _____ Hendrickson worked with a team of divers to excavate a sunken ship.

   _____ Hendrickson helped Franck Goddio uncover Cleopatra's royal quarters.

   _____ The first *Tyrannosaurus rex* skeleton was discovered.

© Rainbow Bridge Publishing

Reading Comprehension • RB-904060

Man with a Dream

On August 28, 1963, over 250,000 people came from all over the United States to march peacefully in Washington, D.C. Their mission was to urge Congress to pass civil rights legislation. They wanted equality for African Americans.

The last speaker that day was Dr. Martin Luther King, Jr. His "I have a dream" speech became one of the most famous speeches ever delivered. To add to the inspiration of the moment, he delivered his speech on the steps of the Lincoln Memorial.

King pleaded for people to judge one another by the content of their character rather than by the color of their skin. He repeatedly used the words "I have a dream . . . " to emphasize the various points of his speech. He used the phrase "Let freedom ring . . . " many times near the end of his speech for the same reason. This powerful speech, delivered in the U.S. capital, played a huge role in getting Congress to pass the Civil Rights Act of 1964.

An articulate, intelligent, and well-respected man, Dr. Martin Luther King, Jr. became a figurehead in the U.S. civil rights movement. In 1954, King became the pastor of a church in Montgomery, Alabama. In 1955, he led the African American boycott of the Montgomery bus system. The boycott began when Rosa Parks refused to give up her seat to a white passenger. In the end, the boycott was successful. The Supreme Court ruled segregation on buses as unconstitutional.

King spoke on the subjects of civil rights and equality over 2,500 times. He and his staff participated in numerous demonstrations and protests in many southern cities. King advocated peaceful protests and demonstrations as a means to achieve change. In 1964, at the age of 35, Dr. Martin Luther King, Jr. received the Nobel Peace Prize.

Reading Comprehension

1. Which of these cities was the setting for King's famous "I Have a Dream" speech?
   A. New York City, New York
   B. Memphis, Tennessee
   C. Birmingham, Alabama
   D. Washington, D.C.

2. Which of the following events happened first?
   A. King received the Nobel Peace Prize.
   B. King delivered his "I Have a Dream" speech.
   C. King became a Baptist minister in Alabama.
   D. King led the bus boycott in Montgomery, Alabama.

3. Which of the following best defines the type of equality that Dr. King championed?
   A. gender
   B. economic
   C. racial
   D. age

4. Which of these statements is an opinion?
   A. King's "I have a dream" speech is the most powerful speech ever delivered.
   B. King's "I have a dream" speech was delivered on the steps of the Lincoln Memorial.
   C. King led the bus boycott in Montgomery, Alabama.
   D. King received the Nobel Peace Prize in 1964.

5. Why do you think Dr. Martin Luther King, Jr. emphasized that protests and demonstrations should not involve violence?

   _____

   _____

   _____

   _____

© Rainbow Bridge Publishing

Two Years in Hiding

When the Nazi party came to power in Germany in the 1930s, Hitler launched a campaign against Jewish people and other European and North African minority groups. The Jewish-German family of Otto Frank began to fear for their future in Germany. Otto then left Germany for Amsterdam, in the Netherlands. There, he started a new business, and his family joined him a short time later.

When the Germans invaded the Netherlands, the Franks were once again forced to live under Nazi rule. Anti-Semitic *decrees* were announced. The Frank family feared for their lives, and they decided to go into hiding. The Franks and four other people hid in the annex above Otto's business. During their 25 months in hiding, 13-year-old Anne Frank kept a journal. In her journal, Anne wrote candidly about her family and their life in hiding. In spite of the oppressive conditions, Anne maintained a positive attitude, writing that "in spite of everything, I still believe that people are truly good at heart."

In August of 1944, an unknown informant betrayed Anne, her family, and their companions. They were arrested and deported to Nazi concentration camps. In 1945, nine months after her arrest, 15-year-old Anne Frank died of typhus at Bergen-Belsen. She died only a few weeks before the concentration camp was liberated by British troops. Otto was the only member of the Frank family who survived the war.

Anne's diary was saved during the war by one of the family's helpers. Miep Gies gave the pages of Anne's diary to Otto after he returned to Amsterdam. He had them published in memory of his daughter. Anne's diary has since been translated into 67 languages. It is one of the most widely read books in the world.

Reading Comprehension

1. Why did the Frank family go into hiding?
   A. They wanted to protect Anne's diary.
   B. They feared being prosecuted for crimes committed in Germany.
   C. They feared for their lives.
   D. They did not get along well with their neighbors.

2. How was the Frank family's hiding place discovered?
   A. A customer in Otto's business heard them upstairs.
   B. They were betrayed by an unknown informant.
   C. Hitler knew where Jewish citizens were located.
   D. Miep Gies accidentally let their location slip in a conversation.

3. Which of the following best defines the word *decrees?*
   A. orders
   B. checks
   C. papers
   D. requests

4. Which of the following events happened second?
   A. Otto Frank started a business in Amsterdam, Netherlands.
   B. Hitler's Nazi party came to power in Germany.
   C. Anne Frank began to keep a journal.
   D. The Frank family went into hiding.

5. Why do you think the words Anne Frank recorded during her family's months in hiding have become so widely read?

   _____

   _____

   _____

   _____

   _____

The Berlin Wall

After World War II, Germany became a divided nation. Sections of Germany under the control of the United States, France, and Britain formed the Federal Republic of Germany (West Germany). The land controlled by the Soviet Union became the German Democratic Republic (East Germany). In no place was the country's division seen more clearly than in the city of Berlin, where a wall was built to separate the two nations.

The borders between East and West Germany were closed in 1952. However, because both nations claimed parts of Berlin, the border in the city was left open. However, in 1961 East Germany began blocking off East Berlin from West Berlin. People living in East Berlin were no longer permitted to cross over into West Berlin.

Prior to the building of the wall, East Berlin was a part of East Germany, and was under Communist control. Many of the people living in East Germany were unhappy with the conditions there. Rules restricted their freedoms. There were no such rules on the other side of the city. Thousands crossed over to the freedom and capitalism of West Berlin. The government of East Germany built the wall to stop this *exodus* to the West.

The Berlin Wall became a system of barriers. Over 96 miles (155.5 km) of barbed wire fence enclosed the city of West Berlin. A concrete wall was erected that stood over 11 feet (3.4 m) high. Security around the wall on the eastern side included watchdogs, patrol trucks, watchtowers, a second wall, and a trench to prevent vehicles from breaking through. Anyone caught in between the two walls was shot without warning. Over 160 people who tried to escape were killed at the Berlin Wall, and another 200 were injured.

As the years went by, the leaders of East Berlin's Communist Party decided to allow some people to cross into West Berlin to visit relatives. Before long, hundreds of other East Berliners wanted to leave, too. In response to the growing pressure, the wall was torn down in 1989. This reunited East and West Berlin and paved the way for German reunification. Today, a painted red line marks where the wall once stood. A few sections of the Berlin Wall remain standing as a memorial.

© Rainbow Bridge Publishing *Reading Comprehension* • RB-904060

Reading Comprehension

1. In which country are East and West Berlin located?
   A. France
   B. Germany
   C. Spain
   D. Italy

2. Which of the following best defines the word *exodus*?
   A. large gathering
   B. mass departure
   C. arrival of many at the same time
   D. attending a major event

3. Why was the Berlin Wall built?
   A. to make Berlin a more beautiful place to live
   B. to please the people who lived in West Berlin
   C. to prevent residents of East Berlin from crossing into West Berlin
   D. to prevent racial integration

4. Which of the following events happened first?
   A. The concrete wall was built.
   B. Some trips to West Berlin were allowed by the Communist Party.
   C. Thousands of East Berlin's residents became dissatisfied with East Berlin and crossed into West Berlin.
   D. A red line was painted to mark where the wall once stood.

5. What other barrier compares to the Berlin Wall? Explain your answer.

   _____

   _____

   _____

   _____

   _____

   _____

© Rainbow Bridge Publishing   *Reading Comprehension* • RB-904060

The Play's the Thing

Belle of the Ball: A Comedy in Two Acts
by Elizabeth Weaver

Cast: (in order of appearance)

Elizabeth Brown . . . . Lucy Scott

Belle Brown . . . . Meg Mitchell

Dressmaker . . . . Susan Moore

Mr. Brown . . . . Grant Jordan

Mrs. Brown . . . . Jennifer Mills

Dr. Gregory Reid. . . . . Shawn Stevens

Ernest Enderby . . . . Michael Thompson

Clover, the family cat . . . . Clover

Partygoers: Bryan Abbot, Ben Adams, Ann Davis, Brooke Harris, Grace Jones, Chandra King, Joe Lee, Andy Miller, Susan Moore, Hugh Young

ACT I

Time: mid-afternoon

Setting: 1920s, the Brown family home

Elizabeth and Belle Brown are in their *boudoir* getting ready for their family's annual ball. The dressmaker is trying to accommodate Elizabeth's unreasonable demands. Belle is quietly putting the finishing touches on her dress. Mr. and Mrs. Brown converse with Dr. Reid and Ernest Enderby. The girls enter the room. Clover, the family cat, emerges from his hiding place under the sofa.

ACT II

Time: evening

Setting: the ballroom

Elizabeth and Belle mingle with the partygoers. Belle leads the dancing until the ball is unexpectedly disrupted. The guests gather outside. Ernest Enderby makes an announcement.

© Rainbow Bridge Publishing *Reading Comprehension* • RB-904060

Reading Comprehension

1. Based on the information in the playbill, do you think you would enjoy this play? Explain your answer.

   _____

   _____

   _____

   _____

2. Which actor plays more than one role?
   A. Grant Jordan
   B. Lucy Scott
   C. Susan Moore
   D. Walter Bennett

3. Why might it be difficult for an actor to play more than one role?

   _____

   _____

   _____

4. Which of the following best defines the word *boudoir*?
   A. a small shop located on the edge of town
   B. a cellar used for storage space
   C. decorations for a party
   D. a woman's dressing room

5. What is the setting for Act II? _____

6. The acts in a play are often divided into smaller segments called scenes. On a separate sheet of paper, write a scene for one of the acts in *Belle of the Ball.*

© Rainbow Bridge Publishing

The Smithville Gazette

Amusement Park Not Fun for Everyone

June 16, 2006—The towering roller coasters of Smithville's new amusement park have brought excitement, tourists, and increased *revenue* to the city. However, in a written noise complaint filed yesterday with the city council, Smithville resident Martha Bergman publicized her displeasure with the amusement park. Bergman wrote, "The roller coasters don't stop running until midnight on the weekdays, and, on weekends, it's one o'clock before the noise stops. I wake up for work at six in the morning. The amusement park prevents me from getting the sleep I need. I'm exhausted!"

Bergman has lived in her house for 26 years.

Lotsa-Fun Company, which owns and operates the Smithville Multi-Fun Amusement Park, bought most of the park's land from area homeowners. When Bergman refused to sell her home, the company was forced to build beside her lot.

Reginald Sampson, the park's general manager, says that his company dealt fairly with Bergman. "We saw how attached she was to her house," Sampson said, "so we made her a very generous offer for her property. She wouldn't take it. She knew what she was getting into; it's not like we kept the plans for the amusement park a secret."

Original blueprints for the site show a roller coaster near the location of Bergman's house. According to Sampson, the park's developers redesigned the site when Bergman would not sell. Now, a parking lot separates her house from the park.

The park's location was debated in five city council meetings. Bergman attended all of them. Bergman said, "I love this house, and I don't want to have to move, but the Multi-Fun Amusement Park is making me miserable."

In response to Bergman's comments, city council member Louise O'Neil said, "We will take Ms. Bergman's complaint seriously and discuss the matter at our next meeting. Hopefully, we can find a solution that will make everyone happy."

Reading Comprehension • RB-904060

Reading Comprehension

1. Choose another good title for the reading.
   A. Resident Not Amused by Park
   B. A Smithville Resident Is Exhausted
   C. That's Just Silly!
   D. Hooray for Lotsa-Fun!

2. Which of the following best defines the word *revenue*?
   A. traffic
   B. crime
   C. income
   D. respect

3. Why does Reginald Sampson say that Martha Bergman should not complain about the new amusement park?

   _____

   _____

   _____

4. Martha Bergman is upset because
   A. the heavy traffic caused by the amusement park often makes her late for work.
   B. the roller coasters block the view from her kitchen window.
   C. the noise from the park keeps her awake at night.
   D. the Lotsa-Fun company did not want to buy her house.

5. Imagine that you are a member of the Smithville City Council. What suggestions would you offer to help resolve this issue?

   _____

   _____

   _____

   _____

   _____

© Rainbow Bridge Publishing   *Reading Comprehension • RB-904060*

Alcatraz

Alcatraz is a 22-acre island located 1.5 miles (2.4 km) offshore in the San Francisco Bay. Spanish explorers named the island Alcatraces, a word usually defined as meaning "pelican." The United States gained possession of the island following the Mexican-American War in 1848. When the California gold rush raised government concerns about a possible attack by pirates, army engineers built a fort on Alcatraz to protect the bay.

During the Civil War, Alcatraz was used to store Union weapons. Later, when the Great Depression ushered in an era of organized crime, the nation needed a maximum-security prison to house its most *incorrigible* offenders. Alcatraz was chosen because of its isolation.

Alcatraz was renovated, and security measures were increased to ensure that no prisoner could escape. The cold waters surrounding the prison made escape even more difficult. Wardens from the nation's other prisons were invited to send their most difficult inmates. Inmates included Al Capone, George Kelly, and Robert Stroud, the "Birdman of Alcatraz."

Records say that no inmate successfully escaped from Alcatraz. Thirty-six inmates tried. All of the escapees were either caught or killed except for five, who are presumed to have drowned. High maintenance costs and an increasing emphasis on rehabilitation rather than simple imprisonment caused the prison to close in 1963. Today, it remains one of San Francisco's main tourist attractions. Several boatloads of passengers tour the island every day.

Reading Comprehension • RB-904060

Reading Comprehension

1. Which of the following is not true of Alcatraz?
   A. Its original name is usually defined as meaning "pelican."
   B. It was used as a maximum-security prison.
   C. It was attacked by pirates during the California gold rush.
   D. It was used to store Union weapons during the Civil War.

2. Which best pinpoints the location of the island of Alcatraz?
   A. off the coast of southern California
   B. in San Francisco Bay
   C. near Ellis Island in New York
   D. in the Gulf of Mexico

3. Why was Alcatraz chosen as the site for a maximum-security prison?
   A. its isolated location
   B. its highly trained staff of guards
   C. its state-of-the-art design
   D. its proximity to other federal prisons

4. Which of the following best defines the word *incorrigible*?
   A. offensive and rude
   B. unable to be reformed
   C. lazy and uncooperative
   D. unhealthy

5. If there are no indications that anyone ever successfully escaped, why did authorities close Alcatraz?

   _____

   _____

   _____

   _____

© Rainbow Bridge Publishing *Reading Comprehension* • RB-904060

Myths, Legends, and Folktales

Many people use the words "myth," "legend," and "folktale" interchangeably. However, each type of story has basic characteristics. Readers can use these characteristics to figure out the *genres* of their favorite stories.

A myth is an important part of the culture that created it. Myths are a way of explaining how the world, a particular custom, or natural phenomenon came to exist. Later cultures do not believe the myth to be true. Myths often feature powerful gods or heroes; myths about regular, average people are rare. Because they often have gods in them, a culture's myths are also a part of their religion. Examples of myths include stories from Greek mythology, such as that of Medusa or Hercules.

Legends are different from myths in that legends do not include the supernatural. While myths contain gods and monsters as characters, legends are about people who may have actually lived. Legends can be very realistic or slightly unbelievable, but you could never say, "That's impossible!" about a legend. Legends usually teach their listeners a lesson or have a moral, which is one reason why people enjoy telling them. Examples of legends include stories about King Arthur and his knights.

Folktales are the trickiest of the three genres to define. Even folklorists have trouble defining what a folktale is, and their jobs are to study folktales! A folktale is a story that primarily exists in the oral tradition. Usually it is more fun to hear a folktale than to read it. The way the storyteller acts out the story can be very entertaining. Folktales fall between myths and legends when it comes to being realistic. Even though folktales do not include gods or heroes, they are still unbelievable. For example, many folktales contain talking animals. Folktales are designed to be fun to listen to, but they still teach good behavior and morals. Examples of folktales are stories about Paul Bunyan and his blue ox, Babe.

Reading Comprehension

1. Which of the following would best be described as a folktale?
   A. the story of a half-bull, half-man that lives in a maze
   B. the story of Little Red Riding Hood
   C. the story of William Tell
   D. the story of a woman whom a god changed into a spider

2. Which of the following is not a reason someone would tell a myth?
   A. to explain why the sky is blue
   B. to explain where a mountain came from
   C. to explain why children should respect their parents
   D. to explain why leaves change colors during the fall

3. Which of the following best defines the word *genres*?
   A. a French word for "myths"
   B. specific kinds of folktales that come from the United States
   C. people who study myths, legends, and folktales
   D. categories or types

4. Which of the following is true of a legend?
   A. Legends feature characters who never could have lived.
   B. Legends often teach a lesson or have a moral.
   C. Legends are no longer told today.
   D. Legends explain how the world, a particular custom, or a natural phenomenon came to exist.

5. Think of a story that you like. Would this story fall into any of these categories? Explain your answer.

   _____

   _____

   _____

   _____

© Rainbow Bridge Publishing *Reading Comprehension* • RB-904060

Conquering Mount Everest

At 29,028 feet (8847.7 m) above sea level, Mount Everest is the world's tallest mountain. The mountain, located in Nepal, was named in honor of Sir George Everest, the British surveyor general of India. Summer monsoons and winter storms usually limit attempts to climb Everest to the months of May and October. There is very little oxygen at that height, and wind speeds can reach over 100 miles (160.9 km) per hour.

In 1924, two members of a British expedition, George Mallory and Andrew Irvine, attempted to reach the summit. The two men were sighted near the top. Clouds then covered the view, and the climbers simply vanished. Mallory's body was not discovered until many years later, and Irvine's body is still missing. No one knows if the pair actually reached the summit of the mountain.

In 1953, New Zealand native Sir Edmund Hillary and Tenzing Norgay, a Sherpa climber, did actually reach the summit. They are credited with being the first to reach the top of the mountain and return safely.

Peter Habeler and Reinhold Messner were climbers who did not believe in using supplemental oxygen. After scaling several other landmark mountains around the world, they set their sights on Mount Everest. They failed in their first attempt. However, they tried a second time and in 1978 reached the summit without supplemental oxygen, an achievement that had been considered impossible. Since then, several others have accomplished the same feat.

Almost 2,250 people from over 20 countries have successfully climbed Mount Everest. Over 180 climbers have lost their lives trying. For those seeking adventure, there are now guided expeditions up the mountain. The only requirements are that the climber be in good physical shape and have the required $65,000 or more to cover the costs of the trip.

© Rainbow Bridge Publishing

Reading Comprehension

1. Why do you think so many climbers are willing to risk their lives to climb Mount Everest?

   _____

   _____

   _____

2. Which of these statements is true?
   A. Wind speeds at the summit of Mount Everest can reach over 100 miles (160.9 km) per hour.
   B. George Mallory and Tenzing Norgay became the first climbers to reach the top of Mount Everest and return safely.
   C. Andrew Irvine made the first successful climb without supplemental oxygen.
   D. Mount Everest expeditions are open only to professional climbers.

3. What was unique about the climb of Habeler and Messner?
   A. They climbed the mountain in December.
   B. They reached the top from the opposite side.
   C. They reached the summit without using supplemental oxygen.
   D. They were the first to ski down the mountain.

4. What obstacles make climbing Mount Everest a difficult thing to do?

   _____

   _____

   _____

5. Today, guided expeditions up Mount Everest cost over $65,000. Why do you think the trip is so expensive?

   _____

   _____

   _____

© Rainbow Bridge Publishing

The Watergate Scandal

In June of 1972, trouble was brewing in Washington, D.C. Five men were arrested for breaking into the headquarters of the Democratic National Committee. The office was a part of the Watergate hotel and office complex. Two White House aides were implicated, but President Richard Nixon, a Republican, denied any knowledge of the break-in. Even though members of President Nixon's staff had taken part in the crime, no one could prove that President Nixon himself had anything to do with it.

However, two reporters who worked for the *Washington Post* discovered a conspiracy behind the incident. Their names were Carl Bernstein and Bob Woodward. The reporters were able to expose the cover-up because a secret source in the U.S. government gave them inside information. If the president found out who the informant was, the source would have lost his job, so Bernstein and Woodward called him "Deep Throat" to protect his identity. When they made their discovery public, the nation was shocked. A special committee was created to investigate the matter.

Some of President Nixon's former personnel testified that he knew about the break-in. They said that he tried to cover up evidence. Confidence in the president sank to a new low. When it became obvious that he would be *impeached*, President Nixon chose to resign from the presidency. President Nixon remains the only president to resign from office. His successor to the presidency, Gerald Ford, granted Nixon a pardon, meaning that Nixon could not be put on trial for his illegal activities.

President Nixon's resignation effectively ended the Watergate scandal, but the identity of Deep Throat remained a secret. Finally, on May 31, 2005, the man who called himself Deep Throat revealed his identity. The informant, William Mark Felt, had been one of the most powerful people in the FBI during President Nixon's administration. Woodward and Bernstein confirmed that Felt was indeed the man who helped crack the Watergate conspiracy. While some people think that Felt betrayed his president, many believe that he did the right thing by exposing corruption in the government.

© Rainbow Bridge Publishing

Reading Comprehension • RB-904060

Reading Comprehension

1. Number the following events in the order that they happened.

    _____   President Nixon resigned from office.

    _____   Five men were arrested for breaking into the headquarters
                of the Democratic National Committee.

    _____   Acting on a tip from a source they called Deep Throat, two
                reporters exposed the cover-up.

    _____   William Mark Felt admitted that he was Deep Throat.

    _____   President Nixon denied any knowledge of the break-in.

2. Which of the following best defines the word *impeached*?
   A. charged with misconduct
   B. made fun of
   C. spoken to sharply
   D. resigned

3. President Nixon resigned from office. Why is this notable?

   _____

   _____

   _____

4. Why did Carl Bernstein and Bob Woodward protect the identity of
   their informant?

   _____

   _____

   _____

5. Do you think William Mark Felt did the right thing by exposing the
   president's involvement in the break-in? Why or why not?

   _____

   _____

   _____

© Rainbow Bridge Publishing *Reading Comprehension* • RB-904060

Who Discovered America?

In the United States, October 12 is often celebrated as the day when Columbus discovered America. Every student in the United States knows the story well. However, many people now believe that another European discovered North America nearly 500 years before Columbus arrived.

Many people believe that the first European explorer to come to America was Leif Erikson. He was the son of Eric the Red, an adventurer originally from Norway. Eric the Red was *exiled* from his home in Iceland for three years. During that time, he bought a boat and went in search of land to the west of Iceland. Eric the Red found a huge island, which he named Greenland to encourage people to settle there.

Leif Erikson grew up listening to stories about a land that lay even farther to the west of Greenland. These sagas told of a place that had much of value not available in the cold northern climate of Greenland. Erikson took a small crew and sailed in search of this new land. When he and his men reached the land, they went ashore in three separate places. They found fertile soil, rivers teeming with fish, and thick forests. Erikson was so delighted that he named the land *Vinland*.

His discovery occurred around 1000 A.D. In 1964, the U.S. Congress commemorated Erikson's accomplishment when they authorized President Lyndon B. Johnson to proclaim October 9 as Leif Erikson Day. Now, each year the president of the United States issues the same proclamation.

© Rainbow Bridge Publishing *Reading Comprehension* • RB-904060

Reading Comprehension

1. Which of these statements is false?
   A. Leif Erikson's father was Eric the Red.
   B. Leif Erikson was born in Vinland.
   C. The land called Vinland was really the coast of North America.
   D. Eric the Red discovered Greenland.

2. Which happened last?
   A. Columbus reached America.
   B. Eric the Red discovered Greenland.
   C. Leif Erikson discovered Vinland.
   D. Leif Erikson grew up in Greenland.

3. Why do you think Leif Erikson called the land he discovered *Vinland*?
   A. The name suggested that the land was fertile.
   B. The name sounded ominous.
   C. He wanted to keep the land for himself and his family.
   D. He thought his friends back in Greenland would be impressed.

4. Which of the following best defines the word *exiled*?
   A. banished from one's own country
   B. exhausted from running from the law
   C. given a position of honor in one's own country
   D. unable to perform one's civic duty

5. Why do you think that Leif Erikson's discovery does not receive the same recognition that Christopher Columbus's later discovery of the Americas receives?

   _____

   _____

   _____

   _____

© Rainbow Bridge Publishing   *Reading Comprehension* • RB-904060

Aloha!

In 1959, Hawaii became the United States of America's 50th state. Before Hawaii could become a state, the voters there had to approve the change. A *referendum* was held, and Hawaiians voted overwhelmingly in favor of becoming a U.S. state.

The first people to set foot on the Hawaiian Islands were Polynesian fishermen, who sailed there from other islands in the South Pacific. They arrived by a combination of good luck and an uncanny ability to sail without instruments. The first European to visit the islands was British explorer Captain James Cook, who landed there in the late 1700s. Cook called the islands the Sandwich Islands in honor of his patron, the Earl of Sandwich.

Throughout much of the 1800s, Hawaii was a monarchy with kings and queens. During that time, the sugar and pineapple industries were expanded by capital provided by American businessmen. Queen Liliuokalani tried to introduce a new constitution in 1893. Her plan would have allowed her to regain much of the power that had been lost by recent monarchs. The constitution was not accepted, and she was forced to give up her throne. A provisional government was set up, but this plan was only temporary, as the islands were annexed by the United States in 1898. Soon after, Hawaii became a U.S. territory.

The island chain extends for more than 1,600 miles (2,575 km). There are eight main islands and 124 smaller islets, reefs, and shoals. The islands are composed almost completely of volcanic ash. The main islands are Hawaii, Maui, Kahoolawe, Lanai, Molokai, Oahu, Kauai, and Niihau.

Tourism is by far the most important industry in Hawaii, and thousands of people vacation there every year. The mild temperatures and beautiful scenery make Hawaii a popular destination. The export of pineapple, coffee, sugarcane, orchids, and macadamia nuts also help boost Hawaii's economy.

© Rainbow Bridge Publishing Reading Comprehension • RB-904060

Reading Comprehension

1. Which of the following best defines the word *referendum*?
   A. popular vote on an issue
   B. referral by another
   C. proclamation
   D. recall election

2. All of the following industries are important to Hawaii's economy except
   A. pineapple.
   B. tourism.
   C. sugarcane.
   D. cotton.

3. Which of the following events happened last?
   A. Hawaii became a state.
   B. The Hawaiian Islands became a U.S. Territory.
   C. Captain James Cook called the islands the Sandwich Islands.
   D. Queen Liliuokalani was forced to give up her throne.

4. Fill in the blanks to complete the following sentences.

   In 1959, Hawaii became the United States of America's _____ state.

   The first people to set foot on the Hawaiian Islands were

   _____.

   _____ was the first European to visit the island.

   _____ tried to introduce a new constitution.

   The islands are composed almost completely of _____.

   Hawaii's most important industry is _____.

© Rainbow Bridge Publishing   *Reading Comprehension* • RB-904060

Woodstock 1969

In the United States, the 1960s were a time of revolution. Young people were breaking away from traditional values and beliefs. The nation was divided over the Vietnam War. In the midst of this turmoil, there was a plan to stage the greatest rock concert of all time. The event was originally called "The Woodstock Music and Art Fair," but has since become known simply as Woodstock 1969. Originally, the event was planned to happen in Wallkill, New York. But, the people there wanted no part of the concert, so promoters moved the site to Max Yasgur's 600-acre pasture in Sullivan County in upstate New York.

The concert was scheduled to begin on a Friday afternoon in August and end the next Monday morning. The four young men who put the concert together adopted the slogan of "Three Days of Peace and Music." They knew antiwar protestors would be there, but they wanted the theme of the concert to emphasize peace. Promoters expected a crowd of up to 50,000 people. Before it was over, nearly 10 times that number had been a part of Woodstock 1969.

Traffic on the freeway was backed up for over 20 miles (32.2 km). There were few sanitation facilities and not enough food. Heavy rain turned the pasture into a *quagmire*. People flocked to Woodstock for a variety of reasons. Some came to protest the Vietnam War, while flower children advocated peace and love. Many fun-loving people came just for the music. Thirty-one musical acts appeared on the main stage. Most were famous rock groups and stars.

When it was over, people who attended Woodstock 1969 came away with their own conclusions about the experience. Now, almost 40 years later, people can again come to the site of Woodstock 1969 to hear music. A center for the arts featuring a large music pavilion has been built on the land where one of the greatest rock concerts in history took place.

Reading Comprehension • RB-904060

Reading Comprehension

1. Which was not a problem at Woodstock?
   A. heavy rain
   B. inadequate sanitation facilities
   C. huge traffic jams
   D. insufficient entertainment

2. Which of the following best defines the word *quagmire*?
   A. a quality control program
   B. a soft, muddy mess
   C. a central meeting place
   D. a makeshift jail

3. Which of the following best describes the flower children who came to Woodstock?
   A. florists who sold concert attendees fresh flowers
   B. peaceful young people
   C. children who were there because their parents brought them along
   D. the nickname given to those who were there to entertain

4. Who came to Woodstock 1969?
   A. antiwar protestors   B. flower children
   C. fun-loving young people   D. all of the above

5. The reading describes the inconvenience and discomforts found at Woodstock 1969. Yet, some people came away from the experience with the notion that it had been the greatest time of their lives. What reasons might they give to support this conclusion?

   _____

   _____

   _____

   _____

   _____

© Rainbow Bridge Publishing   *Reading Comprehension* · RB-904060

Chief Joseph

His Indian name was Hin-mah-too-yah-lat-kekt, which meant "thunder traveling to loftier heights," but he was better known as Chief Joseph. His father, Joseph the Elder, maintained a peaceful relationship with the white settlers and their government. However, when gold was discovered on a Nez Perce reservation, the United States federal government took back much of the land it had given to the Native Americans. The Nez Perce Indians were left with only part of their homeland. Joseph the Elder felt betrayed. He denounced the United States and refused to sign a new treaty. When he died in 1871, Chief Joseph was elected as the leader of the Nez Perce Indians.

Chief Joseph inherited a situation that grew worse as more settlers arrived. A federal order was issued, forcing the Nez Perce onto a small reservation in Idaho. Chief Joseph reluctantly led his people out of their homeland toward the Idaho reservation. Angry at being forced from their homeland and wanting revenge for the murders of relatives, a small group of young Nez Perce Indians raided a nearby settlement. Several settlers were killed.

Chief Joseph and his people knew they would be hunted down, so they tried to flee to Canada. Over 2,000 members of the U.S. Cavalry pursued Chief Joseph and his people. What followed was one of the most brilliant military retreats in U.S. history. Chief Joseph led more than 700 of his followers in an effort to escape the U.S. Cavalry. Each time Joseph's people were forced into battle, they managed to escape.

However, less than 40 miles (64.4 km) from the freedom of the Canadian border, Chief Joseph decided to surrender. His people were tired, cold, and hungry. When he surrendered, Chief Joseph said, "I am tired of fighting. . . . It is cold and we have no blankets. The little children are freezing to death. Hear me, my chiefs. I am tired. My heart is sick and sad. From where the sun now stands, I will fight no more forever."

© Rainbow Bridge Publishing　　　*Reading Comprehension* • RB-904060

Reading Comprehension

1. Which of these events happened first?
   A. Chief Joseph surrendered less than 40 miles (64.4 km) from Canada and freedom.
   B. Chief Joseph led his people on a long retreat.
   C. Chief Joseph was elected chief after his father's death.
   D. Gold was discovered on the homeland of the Nez Perce Indians.

2. Which of these statements is true?
   A. Chief Joseph wanted peace with the settlers.
   B. Chief Joseph was belligerent and refused to honor any federal law.
   C. Chief Joseph led a band of 20 Nez Perce warriors on a raid.
   D. Chief Joseph learned his military maneuvers when he served in the U.S. Cavalry.

3. Which offers the best explanation of Chief Joseph's retreat?
   A. He did not want to have his people live on a reservation.
   B. He was trying to escape the pursuing U.S. Cavalry.
   C. He was trying to win back his native homeland from the settlers.
   D. He assumed that the cavalry would eventually wear down.

4. Why do you think Chief Joseph surrendered to the troops when he was less than 40 miles (64.4 km) from the Canadian border and freedom?

   _____

   _____

   _____

   _____

© Rainbow Bridge Publishing

Underwater "Cities"

Around the world, in warm and shallow waters, coral reefs are an underwater delight. A coral reef is like a complex city that supports a dazzling *array* of life—second only to the diversity found in rain forests. The surprising architects of these "cities" are little animals called coral polyps. Usually no bigger than peas, the coral polyps look like tiny flowers and are just as colorful—a garden of yellows, pinks, purples, oranges, blues, and greens.

The coral polyps extract calcium from the seawater around them. They convert the calcium into limestone and form little cups of rock to support their soft bodies. The coral polyps live in colonies with each polyp attached to its neighbor by the skeleton formed by its outer skin. As the polyps grow, they build new cup skeletons on top of the old ones. The limestone formations built by millions of coral polyps are called coral reefs. The structures formed by the polyps may be branches, cups, ripples, discs, fans, or columns. Each different kind of coral grows in a specific pattern.

Coral reefs provide a habitat for many other animals. The reefs are densely populated by an amazing diversity of marine life, including neon-colored fish, moray eels, soft corals, sponges, tube worms, barracudas, sharks, starfish, manta rays, sea turtles, lobsters, crabs, and shrimp.

Coral fossils indicate that coral reefs have existed in the sea for millions of years. The solid appearance of reefs might lead us to think they are permanent. Actually, coral reefs are fragile, carefully balanced ecosystems that are easily threatened. A change in the temperature or quality of the water, or a change in the amount of light that penetrates the water, can kill the coral polyps.

Some destruction of coral reefs may result from natural causes, but humans cause the greatest damage to reefs. Once a reef is damaged, it may never recover. When that happens, the entire coral community is lost.

Reading Comprehension · RB-904060

Reading Comprehension

1. Why are coral reefs described as complex cities?

   _____

   _____

   _____

2. Which of the following best defines the word *array*?
   A. a home for marine animals
   B. an impressive display or variety
   C. a school of brightly colored fish
   D. a specific pattern

3. The diversity of coral reefs is second only to the diversity found in
   A. the Arctic tundra.
   B. the grasslands of Africa.
   C. rain forests.
   D. swamps and wetlands.

4. Why do polyps extract calcium from the seawater around them?

   _____

   _____

   _____

   _____

5. Why do you think it is human activity that does the most harm to coral reefs?

   _____

   _____

   _____

   _____

   _____

Analyzing Poetry

Robert Frost

Over the course of his career, American poet Robert Frost wrote over 25 volumes of poetry, won an unprecedented four Pulitzer Prizes, and became one of the most beloved poets of the twentieth century. In addition to writing, Frost also taught, lectured, and acted as an unofficial poet laureate of the United States. Much of Frost's work, which is often described as *pastoral*, describes the life and landscapes of rural New England, where he lived for much of his life.

Going for Water

THE WELL was dry beside the door,	1
And so we went with pail and can	2
Across the fields behind the house	3
To seek the brook if still it ran;	4
Not loth to have excuse to go,	5
Because the autumn eve was fair	6
(Though chill), because the fields were ours,	7
And by the brook our woods were there.	8
We ran as if to meet the moon	9
That slowly dawned behind the trees,	10
The barren boughs without the leaves,	11
Without the birds, without the breeze.	12
But once within the wood, we paused	13
Like gnomes that hid us from the moon,	14
Ready to run to hiding new	15
With laughter when she found us soon.	16
Each laid on other a staying hand	17
To listen ere we dared to look,	18
And in the hush we joined to make	19
We heard, we knew we heard the brook.	20
A note as from a single place,	21
A slender tinkling fall that made	22
Now drops that floated on the pool	23
Like pearls, and now a silver blade.	24

Reading Comprehension • RB-904060

Reading Comprehension

1. Robert Frost is often described as a pastoral poet. What does *pastoral* mean, and what examples can you find in "Going for Water" that support this description?

   _____

   _____

   _____

   _____

2. Judging from the poem's tone, how do you think the characters feel about having to fetch water from a nearby brook?

   _____

   _____

3. In line 16, the narrator writes, "With laughter when she found us soon." Who is the word "she" referring to?

   _____

4. To what does the narrator compare himself and his companion?
   A. the leafless trees
   B. gnomes
   C. a running brook
   D. a full moon

5. What do you think happened when the characters reached the brook? Write four more lines to tell your ending.

   _____

   _____

   _____

   _____

Reading Comprehension • RB-904060

James Meredith

James Meredith wanted to become the first African American to attend the University of Mississippi. Meredith applied to the university in 1961, but he was not admitted. He applied again, but that application was also rejected. Meredith believed that he had been denied admission because of his race. He filed a lawsuit against the university.

The case received national media coverage. When it was first heard in district court, the judge ruled in favor of the university. Meredith's lawyers appealed the case to a higher court. The *appellate* court ruled in favor of Meredith. Their ruling said that his case involved educational segregation. The University of Mississippi was ordered to accept Meredith's application.

When Meredith started at the university in the fall of 1962, federal marshals were sent to the campus to protect him. A large protest group rioted against him. During the riots, two people were killed. Many others were injured. But, Meredith bravely registered for classes. Federal troops remained on campus to protect him. President Kennedy addressed the nation, saying that Meredith would continue to be protected, regardless of the cost.

Meredith was determined to graduate from college. He received his degree from the university in 1963. Later, he wrote an account of his experiences in a book titled *Three Years in Mississippi*. His story of courage made him a respected hero for many Americans.

Reading Comprehension • RB-904060

Reading Comprehension

1. Why did James Meredith file a lawsuit against the University of Mississippi?
   A. He wanted to get a good education.
   B. It was important to him to get a degree from a state university.
   C. He was determined to overcome racial segregation in education.
   D. He wanted to become a local hero.

2. Which of these events happened next to last?
   A. Meredith applied for admission to the University of Mississippi.
   B. Meredith attended classes at the university under protection of federal marshals.
   C. Meredith graduated from the University of Mississippi.
   D. Meredith wrote a book titled *Three Years in Mississippi*.

3. Which of the following best defines the word *appellate*?
   A. a higher court that can reverse the decision of a lower court
   B. one who is torn between what is right and what is wrong
   C. a court that makes decisions in cases involving discrimination
   D. one who cannot tolerate political control

4. Which of the following statements is false?
   A. James Meredith applied to the University of Mississippi once.
   B. James Meredith published a book about his years at the university.
   C. James Meredith filed a lawsuit against the University of Mississippi.
   D. Federal marshals protected James Meredith when he enrolled for classes at the University of Mississippi.

5. What do you think President Kennedy meant when he said that James Meredith would be protected, "regardless of the cost"?

   _____

   _____

   _____

   _____

   _____

© Rainbow Bridge Publishing   *Reading Comprehension* • RB-904060

Johnny Appleseed

Johnny Appleseed spent nearly 50 years of his life planting apple seeds and developing apple orchards across the United States. Born in 1774, his real name was John Chapman.

Johnny Appleseed dreamed of a land where apple trees grew everywhere and no one was ever hungry. He tried to be kind to everyone he met—even the animals. He slept outdoors and walked barefoot most of the time. He carried a bag of apple seeds on his back and used a tin pot for a hat and for cooking his food. His clothes were usually made from sacks.

When land in the Northwest Territory—which included the Ohio River Valley—was made available to the public, Johnny Appleseed went there to plant his apple seeds. He wandered through the wilderness until he found a good place for an apple orchard. Then, he cleared the land and planted seeds in neat rows.

He sold his trees for whatever settlers had to offer. Sometimes, he received used clothing in payment, but the clothing he received was usually not the right size. That did not matter to Johnny Appleseed. Over the course of his lifetime, he planted hundreds of *nurseries* and walked thousands of miles across the United States. Some of the trees he planted still bear apples after more than 150 years!

Johnny Appleseed was a great storyteller, and people welcomed him wherever he went. He especially loved children and enjoyed sharing his stories with them. He died in 1845, but the legend of Johnny Appleseed lives on, etched into the history of the United States.

Reading Comprehension • RB-904060

Reading Comprehension

1. Which provides the best explanation for the deeds of Johnny Appleseed?
   A. He thought apple trees were great for providing shade.
   B. He had nothing better to do with his time.
   C. He wanted apple trees everywhere so that no one would be hungry.
   D. He was hired by the federal government to create apple orchards.

2. Where did Johnny Appleseed plant most of his apple trees?
   A. Arizona and New Mexico
   B. Louisiana, Mississippi, and Alabama
   C. Illinois, Indiana, Kentucky, Pennsylvania, and Ohio
   D. upper New York State and New England

3. Which of the following best defines the word *nurseries*?
   A. places where young trees are grown
   B. a place where apple cider is made
   C. a place where young animals are raised
   D. poems for children

4. Which of the following statements is true?
   A. Johnny Appleseed sold the trees he raised for a large profit.
   B. Johnny Appleseed pretended to be poor so people would give him free food and clothing.
   C. Some of Johnny Appleseed's trees still bear fruit after 150 years.
   D. Johnny Appleseed traveled extensively along the East Coast.

5. Why do you think the legend of Johnny Appleseed is still told today?

   _____

   _____

   _____

   _____

© Rainbow Bridge Publishing   *Reading Comprehension* • RB-904060

Maria Montessori

Maria Montessori created and nurtured an entirely new concept in education. After graduating from medical school in Italy—the first woman to do so—she began her own private medical practice. She also worked in a children's hospital and became interested in observing how children learn. She began to think that children teach themselves based on what they find in their environment.

Montessori changed her focus to psychology. She gave up her medical practice to run a small school in Rome for challenged youth. She was not totally surprised when these somewhat unruly children began responding to her methods. She again came to the conclusion that children teach themselves. She found that children absorbed knowledge from their surroundings and had a high natural interest in manipulating materials.

Montessori thought that learning should take place in classrooms where children are not all the same age. She believed that children would learn from one another. Her *developmentally appropriate* methods were designed to fit the needs of each child instead of making each child fit the program. She summed up her thoughts on education with these words: "Never help a child with a task at which he feels he can succeed."

Montessori came to the United States and began training teachers to use her methods. Montessori teachers believe that children learn more by touching, seeing, smelling, tasting, and exploring than by listening. The Montessori teaching method aims to encourage students' creativity, foster independence, and develop social and time management skills.

© Rainbow Bridge Publishing

Reading Comprehension

1. Choose another good title for this story.
   A. Unusual Methods
   B. A New Concept in Education
   C. Teaching in the United States
   D. Fitting into the Program

2. Which of the following senses would be emphasized the least in a Montessori school?
   A. smelling
   B. touching
   C. tasting
   D. listening

3. Which of the following phrases could be a banner on a wall in a Montessori school?
   A. Winning is important!
   B. Children should be seen and not heard.
   C. Creating tomorrow's thinkers today.
   D. Learning to listen, listening to learn.

4. Which of the following best defines the phrase *developmentally appropriate*?
   A. complicated beyond reason
   B. designed to assist growth
   C. convenient and easy
   D. assigned learning

5. What do you think are some of the benefits and drawbacks of the Montessori teaching method?

   _____

   _____

   _____

   _____

© Rainbow Bridge Publishing

Reading Comprehension · RB-904060

Sooners

The most competitive land run in United States history took place at noon on September 16, 1893. On that day, Oklahoma's Cherokee Strip was up for grabs to whoever could get there first. The land to be settled was a strip in northwestern Oklahoma that extended 226 miles (363.6 km) from east to west and 58 miles (93.3 km) from north to south.

Originally, the land had been "given" to the Cherokee tribe by the U.S. government in 1835. It was called the Cherokee Outlet, but the Cherokees never actually lived there. Then, in 1866, the government asked the Cherokees to sell part of the land to other Native American tribes. Several cattle trails also ran across the land as ranchers drove their cattle from Texas to railroads in Kansas. The most famous of these was the Chisholm Trail.

In 1883, an association of ranchers leased five million acres of the rich prairie grasslands from the Cherokees to be used for grazing cattle. Seven years later, President Benjamin Harrison ordered that all of the cattle be removed from the strip as plans were being made to open the land to pioneers.

People came from everywhere to claim a share. Many of them were poor, but they came with dreams of staking their own claims and becoming landowners. President Grover Cleveland beefed up security to eliminate those who would sneak in early. Homesteaders also paid filing fees in advance to try to avoid confusion. These eager settlers gladly paid between $1.00 and $2.50 per acre, depending on the quality of the land. But, the right to homestead the properties would be decided by whoever could get there first. Soldiers were stationed along the starting line to preserve the noontime start.

Some people did jump the gun—they were called "sooners." A few of the sooners were tracked down and caught. At noon, the official gun was fired, and 100,000 pioneers raced to claim 42,000 parcels of land. By sunset, all of the land had been claimed, bringing an end to one of America's last frontiers.

© Rainbow Bridge Publishing

Reading Comprehension

1. Which best identifies the setting for this reading?
   A. Kansas City
   B. northeastern Oklahoma
   C. northwestern Oklahoma
   D. Texas

2. Which of these analogies best characterizes how the land in the Cherokee Strip was awarded to anxious settlers?
   A. a horse race
   B. a cattle call
   C. a wrestling match
   D. a prize drawing

3. Which best describes the land given away on the Cherokee Strip?
   A. fertile farmland
   B. prairie grassland
   C. high desert farmland
   D. mountainous terrain

4. When did the land run described in the reading take place?
   A. early 1800s
   B. late 1800s
   C. early 1900s
   D. none of the above

5. Who were the "sooners"?

   _____

   _____

   _____

   _____

© Rainbow Bridge Publishing

Skin Deep

Chameleons are lizards that have the ability to change color. Nearly half of the more than 100 species of chameleons live on the island of Madagascar. Chameleons are also native to the Middle East, India, and northern Africa.

The skin of a chameleon has cells that contain colored *pigments*. Many people have the mistaken notion that chameleons change colors in response to their surroundings. Chameleons need the ability to be camouflaged for protection against predators, but most species have a basic pattern and color that suits their habitat. In reality, a chameleon's skin changes color in response to temperature, light, and mood.

The various pigments of color are stored within different layers of cells in the skin of the chameleon. The different layers of cells change size, which changes the chameleon's skin color. As the cells enlarge or shrink, the color pigments mix, just like the pigments in paint. For example, a calm chameleon may appear to be green because the yellow cells just beneath the skin's surface in the first layer are contracted. These cells allow blue-reflected light to pass through, and the result is a green appearance. An angry chameleon may appear to be yellow because the surface yellow cells have expanded. These then block the blue-reflected light from below.

Communication is another important reason that chameleons change color. Color may signal that a chameleon is ready to fight or to attract a mate. In the case of the chameleon, beauty is indeed skin deep.

© Rainbow Bridge Publishing

Reading Comprehension

1. What island is home to nearly half of the species of chameleons?
   A. Sri Lanka
   B. Madagascar
   C. Cyprus
   D. Taiwan

2. Color changes in most chameleons occur in response to all of the following except
   A. rainfall.
   B. mood.
   C. temperature.
   D. light.

3. Which of the following best defines the word *pigment*?
   A. diet
   B. environment
   C. inherited trait
   D. tint

4. Which of the following best explains why chameleons change color?
   A. They have an innate love of many different colors.
   B. All lizards have this ability to a certain degree.
   C. They are responding to temperature, light, and mood.
   D. They can better detect the time of day.

5. What other animal do you think should have the ability to change color? Why?

   _____

   _____

   _____

   _____

© Rainbow Bridge Publishing *Reading Comprehension* • RB-904060

Dancing Honeybees

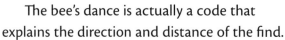

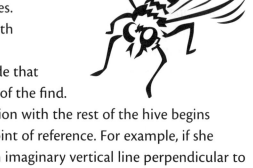

We all know that bees are beneficial because many flowering plants depend on them for pollination. When a honeybee discovers a patch of flowers with *nectar* and pollen, the bee flies back to the hive to alert the other honeybees. The bee dances to communicate with the other bees in the hive.

The bee's dance is actually a code that explains the direction and distance of the find. The honeybee sharing the information with the rest of the hive begins its dance by using the sun as the point of reference. For example, if she performs her dance to the left of an imaginary vertical line perpendicular to the sun, this signals to the other bees that the location of the flowers is to the left of the sun.

An assessment of the size of the find is also included in the dance. A longer dance indicates a good find, while a short dance signals a poor discovery. Within a short period of time, many worker bees have vacated the hive and are headed for the flowers. A honeybee can visit between 50 and 100 flowers during a single collection trip. The average honeybee produces approximately one-twelfth of a teaspoon of honey in her lifetime. It is estimated that bees must visit approximately two million flowers to make one pound of honey.

In each hive, there is a single queen bee, around 20 drones, and approximately 60,000 worker bees. While queen bees can live for three to four years, the average life span of a worker bee is only four to six weeks in the summer and four to six months in the winter. During that time, bees collect nectar to make honey, guard the hive entrance, feed the queen, and help to keep the hive cool by fanning their wings. European honeybees (found all over the world) make more honey than they need, so humans harvest the excess.

Reading Comprehension • RB-904060

Reading Comprehension

1. Which of the following best defines the word *nectar*?
   A. flowers where bees stop and rest
   B. the sweet secretion from flowers
   C. the male bee
   D. the colony's location

2. Which of the following statements is false?
   A. There is only one queen bee in each hive.
   B. Each worker bee can produce approximately one-fourth of a pound of honey in a lifetime.
   C. The length of the dance signifies how good or poor the find is.
   D. When a worker bee finds a patch of flowers, she shares the information with other bees in the hive.

3. Dance movements of the honeybee are coded so that all of the following information about the find is communicated to the other workers except
   A. its direction from the sun.
   B. its approximate distance from the hive.
   C. the size of the discovery.
   D. the risk involved in collecting the nectar.

4. Which of the following best describes the setting for the reading?
   A. all over the world where bees live
   B. western Europe, where bees originated
   C. southern California
   D. Vermont, the bee state

5. In addition to honey, what other useful products are produced by bees or from bee by-products. If necessary, use the Internet or visit your school or local library to search for information.

   _____

   _____

   _____

© Rainbow Bridge Publishing   *Reading Comprehension* · RB-904060

Robert Peary

Robert Peary graduated from college in 1877 and immediately went to work as a surveyor. A short time later, he entered the U.S. Navy Corps of Civil Engineers. It was while he was working in tropical Nicaragua that he began to daydream about exploring the Arctic.

Peary decided to turn his dream into a reality by exploring Arctic lands whenever he was able to get a leave of absence from the navy. He hired civil engineer Matthew Henson as his assistant, and Henson accompanied him on all of his polar explorations.

In 1893, the pair made their first attempt to reach the North Pole. They were able to get within 400 miles (643.6 km) of their goal, but they were then forced to turn back. In 1905, Peary and his team tried again. This time, they pushed their way on *sledges* over the icebound Arctic and came within 175 miles (281.6 km) of their destination. However, they ran short of supplies and turned back again.

Peary and Henson decided to make their next attempt in late winter when the ice was still firm. In early 1909, Peary's crew departed. There were 23 men and 133 dogs. As they traveled, Peary began reducing the size of his party. Finally, on April 6, 1909, Peary, Henson, and four Inuit stood where no man had ever been before—the North Pole.

When the group returned to civilization, Peary learned that another American named Frederick Cook claimed to have reached the North Pole a year before Peary. Two Inuit later testified that they had been with Cook when he staged the fake photographs taken many miles from the North Pole. In 1911, the U.S. Congress formally recognized Peary as the first man to reach the North Pole.

Reading Comprehension

1. Choose another good title for the reading.
   A. North to Alaska
   B. Looking Down at Canada
   C. On Top of the World
   D. First to Freeze

2. What did Congress decide about Frederick Cook's claim to have reached the North Pole before Robert Peary?
   A. Cook's claim was justified.
   B. Cook's claim was false.
   C. There was not enough information to reach a conclusion.
   D. No one will ever know who reached the North Pole first.

3. Which of the following best defines the word *sledges*?
   A. a layer of snow and ice that covers the ground in Arctic regions
   B. a vehicle on runners designed to carry loads or passengers over snow and ice
   C. a domesticated breed of reindeer used by the Inuit for Arctic transportation
   D. a ship designed to break through the ice that blocks waterways

4. Which of the following events happened first?
   A. Peary joined the U.S. Navy.
   B. Peary met Matthew Henson.
   C. Peary was assigned to a project in Nicaragua.
   D. Peary came within 175 (281.6) miles of the North Pole.

5. Robert Peary was once asked how he knew that he had reached the North Pole. His response: "Nothing easier. One step beyond the pole, you see, and the north wind becomes a south one." What do you think Peary meant by this?

   _____

   _____

   _____

   _____

   _____

© Rainbow Bridge Publishing   *Reading Comprehension* • RB-904060

Digital Cameras

The arrival of the digital camera is a breakthrough in technology that is changing the photography industry. While conventional cameras need film that must be developed using chemicals, digital cameras use a built-in computer to record images in an electronic format.

In order for a computer to process an image, the image must first be converted into a format that the computer can recognize. A digital image is really a long string of ones and zeros. These numbers represent all of the tiny colored dots, called *pixels*, of which the image is comprised. To get the image into this format, there are two options.

One option involves using a conventional camera with film. After the photo is printed onto paper, a digital scanner scans the image into pixel values. The other option is to use a digital camera to record the light that bounces off of the subject. These cameras record the image in pixel values immediately, without the use of film.

The digital camera has a light sensor that converts light into electrical charges. There are two kinds of light sensors found in digital cameras. One is used in more expensive cameras. The result is a higher quality image with more pixels that shows a higher sensitivity to light. The other sensor is used in less expensive digital equipment. It results in an image comprised of fewer pixels and a photo of lesser quality.

The amount of detail that a camera can capture is called resolution, and it is measured in pixels. The greater the number of pixels, the more detail will be captured in an image, and the more it can be enlarged without the image becoming distorted. If a photographer wants nothing more than a snapshot to record and store on a computer, the low-end resolution camera is fine. It is also much less expensive. If recording an image of high-resolution quality that can be turned into enlarged photos is desired, then a higher-end camera is needed.

© Rainbow Bridge Publishing *Reading Comprehension* • RB-904060

Reading Comprehension

1. Which of the following best defines the word *pixels*?
   A. colored prints
   B. colored dots
   C. tiny computers
   D. technological language for a completed image

2. Why are the more expensive digital cameras able to deliver better photo images?
   A. Image quality is directly related to the cost of cameras.
   B. The more expensive cameras offer a higher resolution image.
   C. The more expensive cameras filter light through a better lens.
   D. The more expensive cameras record fewer pixels.

3. What is the primary difference between conventional cameras and digital cameras?
   A. the absence of owner control in digital cameras
   B. the quality of the image that results
   C. there is no film in a digital camera
   D. the number of gadgets found in digital equipment

4. To send an image through a computer, that image must first be
   A. translated into a series of Xs and Os.
   B. photocopied.
   C. presented in the language that is recognized by the computer.
   D. sent to a photo lab to make the image ready for delivery.

5. Have you or any of your family members had experience using both a digital camera and a conventional camera? If so, how do the two types of cameras compare? If not, do you think that digital cameras will eventually replace conventional cameras?

   _____

   _____

   _____

   _____

© Rainbow Bridge Publishing   *Reading Comprehension* • RB-904060

Returned to China

Before the British took over, Hong Kong was a small fishing village in the South China Sea. The Opium Wars with China during the nineteenth century brought great change and resulted in Hong Kong being ceded to Britain. Additional conflicts with China resulted in Britain gaining control of Kowloon and Stonecutters Island. In 1898, Britain signed an agreement for a 99-year lease on these lands.

Hong Kong's population grew slowly at first, as exiles from the newly established Chinese Republic began moving to Hong Kong in 1912. However, as the Japanese advanced into China during the 1920s, thousands of Chinese took refuge in Hong Kong. By the time World War II began, the population of Hong Kong had grown to over 1.5 million. During the war, Britain was forced to surrender Hong Kong to the Japanese. When the war ended, Hong Kong was returned to British rule.

During the late 1940s, as the Chinese National Government faced defeat by the communists, hundreds of thousands of Chinese sought refuge in Hong Kong. During the 1950s and 1960s, tax advantages offered by Hong Kong encouraged foreign investors to pour money into Hong Kong's industry. The influx of Chinese immigrants supplied a cheap and available work force that contributed further to its rise in industrial manufacturing.

In more recent times, Hong Kong has grown dramatically in the financial services industries. Social programs continue to raise the standard of living in Hong Kong. The 99-year lease to Britain ended on July 1, 1997. There were huge concerns on both sides about how the transfer of power back to the Chinese would affect Hong Kong. The Sino-British Joint Declaration signed by Britain and China stipulates that the way of life of Hong Kong's citizens will remain unchanged for 50 years, or until 2047. This means that Hong Kong still has a degree of *autonomy* and is not a part of the Chinese socialist system. Its population today is over 6 million.

© Rainbow Bridge Publishing

Reading Comprehension • RB-904060

Reading Comprehension

1. Which of the following factors did not contribute to the rise in Hong Kong's population?
   A. Exiles from China sought refuge in Hong Kong when the Chinese Republic was established.
   B. Refugees from China came to Hong Kong in the 1920s when Japan began invading China.
   C. Thousands of Americans emigrated to Hong Kong for business reasons during World War II.
   D. There was plenty of available work for the Chinese people when foreign investment brought manufacturing jobs to Hong Kong.

2. Which of the following best defines the word *autonomy*?
   A. self-government
   B. rule by a few
   C. rule by a monarch
   D. rule by a dictator

3. What historical incident led to Britain's rule of Hong Kong?
   A. The Joint Declaration
   B. World War II
   C. World War I
   D. The Opium Wars

4. Which of the following happened second?
   A. Britain signed a 99-year lease for control over Hong Kong.
   B. Hong Kong became part of China again on July 1, 1997.
   C. Britain was forced to surrender Hong Kong to the Japanese.
   D. Exiles from the newly established Chinese Republic began moving to Hong Kong.

5. Describe Hong Kong's location in a single well-written sentence. Look at a map if you need help.

_____

_____

© Rainbow Bridge Publishing   *Reading Comprehension* • RB-904060

Arlington National Cemetery

When General Robert E. Lee resigned from the United States Army during the Civil War and assumed command of the Confederate Army, his family was forced to abandon their estate in Arlington, Virginia. During the Civil War, federal troops occupied the property. Many soldiers lost their lives in the heavy fighting in Virginia. General Montgomery Miegs of the Union army suggested that a portion of Arlington be reserved as a cemetery. On June 15, 1864, Secretary of War Edwin M. Stanton declared Arlington House and the land surrounding it a military cemetery.

By the war's end, the fields at Arlington were filled with the graves of fallen soldiers from both the Union and Confederate armies. The neatly arranged rows of headstones were a stark reminder of the cost of the war.

It was another war in 1898 that served as a uniting force between the North and the South. The Spanish-American War did not last long, nor did it take the lives of many American soldiers, but many of the soldiers who died were buried in Arlington National Cemetery. Since then, it has been the most famous cemetery in the United States.

Located on the 200 acres of land surrounding Arlington House, Arlington National Cemetery is the final resting place for veterans of every United States war, including the Revolutionary War. Pre-Civil War veterans were reinterred at Arlington National Cemetery after 1900. Additionally, many notable explorers and historical figures are buried in the cemetery, including President John F. Kennedy and his brother, Senator Robert Kennedy.

Each year, many people who go to Arlington National Cemetery visit the Tomb of the Unknowns, also known as the Tomb of the Unknown Soldier. The unidentified remains of three United States soldiers from World War I, World War II, and the Korean War are interred in this location. The memorial pays *homage* to all of the missing and unidentified service members of the United States armed forces. Sentinels have guarded the Tomb of the Unknowns continuously since July 2, 1937, regardless of inclement weather. They are rotated in hour or half-hour shifts whenever the cemetery is open to the public.

© Rainbow Bridge Publishing

Reading Comprehension

1. Which of the following events happened first?
   A. Arlington House and the land surrounding it was declared a military cemetery.
   B. Sentinels began guarding the Tomb of the Unknowns.
   C. Robert E. Lee resigned from the United States Army.
   D. Veterans from the Spanish-American War were buried at Arlington National Cemetery.

2. Where is Arlington National Cemetery located?
   A. Arlington, Virginia
   B. Yorktown, Virginia
   C. Baltimore, Maryland
   D. Philadelphia, Pennsylvania

3. Which of the following best defines the word *homage*?
   A. to guard and protect
   B. a special honor or show of respect
   C. a grand display that happens yearly
   D. an exhibit that is open to the public

4. How is Montgomery Miegs connected to Arlington National Cemetery?
   A. He bought the property from Custis.
   B. He recommended using the property as a cemetery during the Civil War.
   C. He convinced General Lee to cede the property to the federal government.
   D. He finished the construction project on Arlington House.

5. What role did the Spanish-American War play in the development of Arlington National Cemetery?

   _____

   _____

   _____

   _____

© Rainbow Bridge Publishing

Reading Comprehension • RB-904060

Sonnets

Readers should consider a poem's form when analyzing poetry. Form, or the particular style and structure of a poem, is important because it can provide clues to help readers understand the poem. One of the most famous forms of poetry is the sonnet.

Traditional sonnets have 14 lines and a very complex pattern. Sonnets are often written in iambic pentameter, which is a pattern of stressed and unstressed syllables. There are two main types of sonnets. They can be told apart by their *rhyme schemes*, or the patterns of rhyming words in the poems.

The Italian, or Petrarchan, sonnet is divided into two parts, an eight-line octave and a six-line sestet. The octave can be found at the beginning of the poem. The octave usually states a question, reveals a problem, expresses doubt, or makes a statement about something that happened in the past. The sestet then tries to answer the question, resolve the problem, or respond to the statement or doubt. The rhyme scheme often follows the pattern abba, abba, cdecde or cdcdcd. Because the rhyme scheme of the final six lines can vary, readers must look to the octave to help them determine if a sonnet is an Italian sonnet.

The English, or Shakespearean, sonnet is divided into four parts. The English sonnet has three four-line quatrains, and it concludes with a two-line couplet. Usually, the couplet at the end summarizes the poem or draws it cleverly to a close. The rhyme scheme of an English sonnet is often abab, cdcd, efefgg.

Many famous poets, such as William Shakespeare, have used the sonnet to showcase their talent with language and to discuss difficult or abstract subjects, such as love. To write a sonnet, a poet must also be able to use very precise language within a set rhyme scheme. For these reasons, writing a sonnet is very difficult to do.

Sonnets (continued)

Read the sonnet below and answer the questions (page 70).

Sonnet 29

WHEN in disgrace with fortune and men's eyes	*a*
I all alone beweep my outcast state,	*b*
And trouble deaf heaven with my bootless cries,	*a*
And look upon myself, and curse my fate,	*b*
Wishing me like to one more rich in hope,	*c*
Featur'd like him, like him with friends possess'd,	*d*
Desiring this man's art and that man's scope,	*c*
With what I most enjoy contented least;	*d*
Yet in these thoughts myself almost despising,	*e*
Haply I think on thee—and then my state,	*f*
Like to the lark at break of day arising	*e*
From sullen earth, sings hymns at heaven's gate;	*f*
For thy sweet love remember'd such wealth brings	*g*
That then I scorn to change my state with kings.	*g*

by William Shakespeare

© Rainbow Bridge Publishing   *Reading Comprehension* • RB-904060

Reading Comprehension

1. Which type of sonnet is "Sonnet 29"?

   _____

   How do you know?

   _____

   _____

2. Which of the following is not true of a sonnet?
   A. Traditional sonnets have 14 lines.
   B. There are two main types of sonnets.
   C. Sonnets have a very simple rhyme scheme.
   D. Sonnets are often written in iambic pentameter.

3. Why does William Shakespeare write that he would not change his position with that of a king?

   _____

   _____

   _____

4. Which of the following best defines the phrase *rhyme scheme*?
   A. a pattern of stressed and unstressed syllables
   B. a clever ending to a poem
   C. the particular style and structure of a poem
   D. a pattern of rhyming words

5. On a separate piece of paper, try writing your own sonnet. Choose either the Italian or English type of sonnet. Make sure to follow the appropriate rhyme scheme.

Critical Thinking Skills

The Odd Word Out

Each of the following passages contains at least one word that is used incorrectly. Find and cross out each misused word. Then, write the correct word above each misused word.

1. According to legend, in the Middle Ages, a noble man named Arthur defended England and brought peace to the land. His bravery and goodness won him the love and respect of the English people, and he was crowned president of Camelot. He and his knights were famous for their brave and honorable deeds. They sat at a round table to show that they thought of themselves as equals.

2. Every week, many people around the world go to the movies. For the price of a movie check, they can travel forward or backward in time, join a high-speed car chase, or explore distant galaxies in futuristic spaceships. Movies are certainly a great style of entertainment.

3. Hot air balloons are the oldest type of flight technology. In 1783, the first hot air balloon sunk off the ground in France. It carried a sheep, a chicken, and a duck for about 15 minutes before rising back to Earth. About two months later, two men became the first humans to ride in a hot air balloon. Their flight lasted about 20 minutes. With the success of their ride, the popularity of hot air balloon rides soared to new heights!

4. The hourglass, or sandglass, is one of the first procedures created to measure time. The Greeks used hourglasses as early as 250 B.C. An hourglass is made of two funnel-shaped glass bulbs connected by a narrow neck. Sand slowly gathers from one bulb to the other through the neck. It takes one hour for all of the sand to pass between the bulbs. At the end of one hour, the hourglass may be turned over to start timing a second hour.

© Rainbow Bridge Publishing *Reading Comprehension* • RB-904060

Critical Thinking Skills

Fractured Phrases

Below are several well-known phrases. Draw a line matching the beginning of each phrase with its correct ending. Then, choose three of the phrases and explain what they mean on the lines below.

1. A journey of a thousand miles   wait for no man.

2. If life gives you lemons,   always twenty-twenty.

3. Beauty is in   is not gold.

4. Hindsight is   louder than words.

5. The pen is   make lemonade.

6. Actions speak   the eye of the beholder.

7. Time and tide   by its cover.

8. All that glitters   begins with a single step.

9. A rolling stone   mightier than the sword.

10. Never judge a book   gathers no moss.

11. _____

_____

12. _____

_____

13. _____

_____

© Rainbow Bridge Publishing

Critical Thinking Skills

Oxymorons

An oxymoron is a figure of speech that is created when words with opposite or contradictory meanings are used together. For example, the phrase "jumbo shrimp" is an oxymoron because the word *jumbo* means *large*, and the word *shrimp* is sometimes used to describe things that are very small. Underline the oxymoron in each of the sentences below. Then, on the line provided, explain why the phrase is contradictory.

1. It didn't take long for me to notice that the report I was reading was full of omissions.

   _____

2. The kitten couldn't climb down from the tree, so I had to get a ladder.

   _____

3. The carpenter's measurements were almost exact.

   _____

4. The spilled water in the hallway poses a serious safety hazard.

   _____

5. I called Brad to see if he's coming to the party, and he said that he's a definite maybe.

   _____

6. One of the things I like about Kelly is that she is hopelessly optimistic.

   _____

Reading Comprehension • RB-904060

Critical Thinking Skills

Analogies

Circle the letter of the word that correctly completes each analogy.

1. Stiff is to flexible as empty is to
    A. low.   B. rigid.
    C. full.   D. elastic.

2. Waltz is to dance as oak is to
    A. acorn.   B. tree.
    C. pine.   D. tango.

3. Star is to galaxy as word is to
    A. universe.   B. alphabet.
    C. planet.   D. dictionary.

4. Chapter is to book as an act is to a
    A. novel.   B. comedy.
    C. play.   D. sitcom.

5. Glass is to transparent as wood is to
    A. clear.   B. opaque.
    C. pine.   D. fragile.

6. Laugh is to tickle as shiver is to
    A. cold.   B. bored.
    C. giggle.   D. amused.

7. Thrifty is to miserly as smart is to
    A. cheap.   B. foolish.
    C. gullible.   D. brilliant.

8. Precise is to exact as lively is to
    A. energetic.   B. listless.
    C. inaccurate.   D. quick.

© Rainbow Bridge Publishing *Reading Comprehension* • RB-904060

Rebus Puzzles

A rebus puzzle is a type of puzzle that uses letters, words, and numbers as clues to represent an idea, a popular phrase, or a saying. Often, the placement and size of the "clues" can help convey the puzzle's meaning. Look at the rebus puzzles below. Write the phrase, saying, or idea the clues represent on the line below each puzzle.

1.

Funny   Funny
Words   Words
Words   Words

_____

2.

All world

_____

3.

thodeepught

_____

4.

174safety659

_____

5.

head

heels

_____

6.

time time

_____

© Rainbow Bridge Publishing   *Reading Comprehension* • RB-904060

Critical Thinking Skills

Rebus Puzzles

A rebus puzzle is a type of puzzle that uses letters, words, and numbers as clues to represent an idea, a popular phrase, or a saying. Often, the placement and size of the "clues" can help convey the puzzle's meaning. Look at the rebus puzzles below. Write the phrase, saying, or idea the clues represent on the line below each puzzle.

1.

cut ◄————————

cut   cut   cut
cut   cut   cut

_____

2.

little   little

late   late

_____

3.

PROMISE

_____

4.

the calm the storm

_____

5.

aallll

_____

6.

G H
N   O
S I
R

_____

Answer Key

Page 5, Jesse's Gold

1. A.; 2. C.; 3. A.; 4. C.; 5. Answers will vary. To set records and win gold medals at the Olympics was a huge accomplishment that is only dreamed about by most people.

Page 7, The Rescue of JFK

1. D.; 2. C.; 3. 2, 1, 3, 5, 4; 4. A.; 5. Answers will vary. The coast watchers and scouts were dedicated to the Allied cause and wanted to help the crew in any way possible.

Page 9, The Great Bambino

1. B.; 2. C.; 3. C.; 4. B.; 5. Answers will vary.

Page 11, Analyzing Poetry

1. A.; 2. "She" is the setting sun. Some possible clues include: Dickinson uses the phrase "the Evening West" and the sun sets in the west. She refers to the stars that are becoming visible in the sky, and the colors Dickinson describes are colors found in sunsets.; 3. Answers will vary.; 4. C.; 5. Answers will vary.

Page 13, Billie Jean King

1. 1968; August, 1973; September 20, 1973; 1974; 1984; 2. B.; 3. King proved that female athletes should not be underestimated and that they can thrive in pressure-filled situations.; 4. D.; 5. Answers will vary.

Page 15, Alquerque

1. Answers will vary.; 2. D.; 3. A player's piece must be sitting beside an opponent's piece, and the space beyond the opponent's piece must be empty.; 4. T, F–The game is over when a player has captured all of his opponent's pieces or when no more captures can be made by either player., F–players may choose whether to move again after capturing an opponent's piece., F–Alquerque is similar to checkers., T

Page 17, Sue Hendrickson

1. The *T. rex* skeleton Hendrickson found is the largest, most complete, and best preserved skeleton to date.; 2. B.; 3. A paleontologist studies fossilized plants and animals. An archaeologist studies human history by looking at remains and artifacts.; 4. 1, 3, 4, 5, 2

Page 19, Man with a Dream

1. D.; 2. C.; 3. C.; 4. A.; 5. Answers will vary.

Page 21, Two Years in Hiding

1. C.; 2. B.; 3. A.; 4. A.; 5. Answers will vary.

Page 23, The Berlin Wall

1. B.; 2. B.; 3. C.; 4. C.; 5. Answers will vary. Accept any reasonable answer. From history, the Great Wall of China is a good example.

Answer Key

Page 25, The Play's the Thing
1. Answers will vary.; 2. C.; 3. Answers will vary but may include: More than one role might mean quick costume and makeup changes as well as the challenges of changing characters.; 4. D.; 5. the ballroom; 6. Answers will vary.

Page 27, The Smithville Gazette
1. A.; 2. C.; 3. Bergman refused a generous offer and would not sell her home. Then, the park's developers redesigned the park's layout so that a parking lot separated Bergman's house from the amusement park.; 4. C.; 5. Answers will vary.

Page 29, Alcatraz
1. C.; 2. B.; 3. A.; 4. B.; 5. The isolated location of Alcatraz made it costly to operate and contributed to its closing. An increasing emphasis on rehabilitation was also a factor.

Page 31, Myths, Legends, and Folktales
1. B.; 2. C.; 3. D.; 4. B.; 5. Answers will vary.

Page 33, Conquering Mount Everest
1. Answers will vary.; 2. A.; 3. C.; 4. Answers will vary but may include harsh weather, a lack of oxygen, and high wind speeds.; 5. Answers will vary but the cost of accommodations, guides, permits, transportation, supplies, etc., for such a trip is very expensive. Only the best equipment can be used for these tours to make them as safe as possible.

Page 35, The Watergate Scandal
1. 4, 1, 3, 5, 2; 2. A.; 3. Nixon is the only U.S. president to resign from office.; 4. The informant would have lost his job if his identity was revealed.; 5. Answers will vary.

Page 41, Who Discovered America?
1. B.; 2. A.; 3. A.; 4. A.; 5. Answers will vary but may include the idea that some facts regarding Erikson's discovery have yet to be verified, and Columbus's voyage marked the beginning of colonization in the Americas.

Page 39, Aloha!
1. A.; 2. D.; 3. A.; 4. 50th, Polynesian fishermen, Captain James Cook, Queen Liliuokalani, volcanic ash, tourism

Page 41, Woodstock 1969
1. D.; 2. B.; 3. B.; 4. D.; 5. Answers will vary but may include: Those who were there and enjoyed themselves might describe all of the music groups and entertainers who performed there.

Page 43, Chief Joseph
1. D.; 2. A.; 3. B.; 4. Answers will vary but may include: Chief Joseph had reached the point of exhaustion. His people were cold, hungry, and tired. His spirit was broken.

© Rainbow Bridge Publishing *Reading Comprehension* • RB-904060

Answer Key

Page 45, Underwater "Cities"

1. Like large cities, the structures and inhabitants of coral reefs are very diverse.; 2. B.; 3. C.; 4. They convert the calcium into limestone and form little cups of rock to support their soft bodies.; 5. Answers will vary but may include: Pollution, careless tourists and fishermen, and garbage dumped nearby all damage the delicate reefs.

Page 47, Analyzing Poetry

1. *Pastoral* poetry is concerned with country life, nature, and the rural landscape. Frost describes the landscape, such as the trees, moon, and the running brook. 2. The characters view the experience as an adventure and are not inconvenienced by it.; 3. the moon; 4. B.; 5. Answers will vary.

Page 49, James Meredith

1. C.; 2. C.; 3. A.; 4. A.; 5. Answers will vary.

Page 51, Johnny Appleseed

1. C.; 2. C.; 3. A.; 4. C.; 5. Answers will vary but his good deeds were responsible for many of the apple orchards found today throughout the Midwest.

Page 53, Maria Montessori

1. B.; 2. D.; 3. C.; 4. B.; 5. Answers will vary.

Page 55, Sooners

1. C.; 2. A.; 3. B.; 4. B.; 5. Sooners were settlers who "jumped the gun," and did not wait for the official starting time on the day the government gave away land in Oklahoma's Cherokee Strip.

Page 57, Skin Deep

1. B.; 2. A.; 3. D.; 4. C.; 5. Answers will vary.

Page 59, Dancing Honeybees

1. B.; 2. B.; 3. D.; 4. A.; 5. Answers will vary but may include: medicines, cosmetics, candles and other wax products.

Page 61, Robert Peary

1. C.; 2. B.; 3. B.; 4. A.; 5. A person walking toward the North Pole into the wind would suddenly have the wind coming from a southerly direction as soon as he stepped beyond the pole.

Page 63, Digital Cameras

1. B.; 2. B.; 3. C.; 4. C.; 5. Answers will vary.

Page 65, Returned to China

1. C.; 2. A.; 3. D.; 4. D.; 5. Hong Kong is located on the southeastern coast of China and is bordered to the east, west, and south by the South China Sea.

Page 67, Arlington National Cemetery

1. C.; 2. A.; 3. B.; 4. B.; 5. The Spanish-American War served as a uniting force between the North and South because all of the soldiers were on the same side. It was also a short war that was

Reading Comprehension • RB-904060

Answer Key

Page 67, continued

won by the United States. It raised the spirits of a divided nation.

Page 70, Sonnets

1. "Sonnet 29" is English/Shakespearean. The rhyme scheme and author are both clues.; 2. C.; 3. Because he feels fortunate whenever he thinks of the person whom he is writing the poem about, he is already as happy as a king.; 4. D.; 5. Answers will vary.

Page 71, The Odd Word Out

Answers will vary. Accept any reasonable answer. 1. *President* should be crossed out and replaced with *king*.; 2. *Check* should be crossed out and replaced with *ticket*. *Style* should be crossed out and replaced with *form* or *type*.; 3. *Sunk* should be crossed out and replaced with *rose* or *lifted*. *Rising* should be crossed out and replaced with *settling* or *sinking*. 4. *Procedures* should be crossed out and replaced with *instruments*. *Gathers* should be crossed out and replaced with *passes* or *flows*.

Page 72, Fractured Phrases

1. A journey of a thousand miles begins with a single step.; 2. If life gives you lemons, make lemonade.; 3. Beauty is in the eye of the beholder.; 4. Hindsight is always twenty-twenty.; 5. The pen is mightier than the sword.; 6. Actions speak louder than words.; 7. Time and tide wait for no man.; 8. All that glitters

Page 72, continued

is not gold.; 9. A rolling stone gathers no moss.; 10. Never judge a book by its cover.; 11–13. Answers will vary.

Page 73, Oxymorons

1. full of omissions: *full* means to have as much as possible and *omissions* means that something has been left out; 2. climb down: *climb* is an upward motion which is the opposite of *down*.; 3. almost exact: *almost* means not exactly, while *exact* is very precise.; 4. safety hazard: *safety* implies no danger, while a *hazard* is something that threatens safety; 5. definite maybe: *definite* is absolute, while *maybe* indicates uncertainty.; 6. hopelessly optimistic: *hopelessly* means "without hope" while *optimistic* means "to have hope."

Page 74, Analogies

1. C.; 2. B.; 3. D.; 4. C.; 5. B.; 6. A.; 7. D.; 8. A.

Page 75, Rebus Puzzles

1. too funny for words; 2. a small world after all; 3. deep in thought; 4. safety in numbers; 5. head over heels; 6. time after time

Page 76, Rebus Puzzles

1. a cut above the rest; 2. too little, too late; 3. broken promise; 4. the calm before the storm; 5. all in all; 6. horsing around